PAPER CRAFTS FOR EASTER

Randel McGee

Enslow Elementary

an imprint of

Enslow Publishers, Inc.

40 Industrial Road
Box 398
Berkeley Heights, NJ 07922
USA

http://www.enslow.com

Dedicated to the memories of Gertrude "Trudy" Herrmann Evans and Bert P. Evans, my in-laws, for their constant support and encouragement. This holiday celebrates our great expectations!

This book meets the National Standards for Arts Education.

Enslow Elementary, an imprint of Enslow Publishers, Inc.
Enslow Elementary® is a registered trademark of Enslow Publishers, Inc.

Library of Congress Cataloging-in-Publication Data

McGee, Randel.
    Paper crafts for Easter / Randel McGee.
       p. cm. — (Paper craft fun for holidays)
    Includes bibliographical references and index.
    Summary: "Explains the significance of Easter and how to make Easter-themed crafts out of paper"—Provided by
      publisher.
    ISBN 978-0-7660-3723-6
    1. Easter decorations—Juvenile literature. 2. Paper work—Juvenile literature. I. Title.
    TT900.E2M354 2010
    745.594'1—dc22

                  2010013613

Paperback ISBN: 978-1-59845-335-5

Printed in the United States of America

052011 Lake Book Manufacturing, Inc., Melrose Park, IL

10 9 8 7 6 5 4 3 2 1

To Our Readers: We have done our best to make sure all Internet Addresses in this book were active and appropriate when we went to press. However, the author and the publisher have no control over and assume no liability for the material available on those Internet sites or on other Web sites they may link to. Any comments or suggestions can be sent by e-mail to comments@enslow.com or to the address on the back cover.

Every effort has been made to locate all copyright holders of material used in this book. If any errors or omissions have occurred, corrections will be made in future editions of this book.

♻ Enslow Publishers, Inc., is committed to printing our books on recycled paper. The paper in every book contains 10% to 30% post-consumer waste (PCW). The cover board on the outside of each book contains 100% PCW. Our goal is to do our part to help young people and the environment too!

Illustration Credits: Crafts prepared by Randel McGee; photography by Nicole diMella/Enslow Publishers, Inc.

Cover Illustration: Crafts prepared by Randel McGee; photography by Nicole diMella/Enslow Publishers, Inc.

CONTENTS

AUTHOR'S NOTE: Many of the materials used in making these crafts may be found by using recycled paper products. The author uses such recycled items as cereal boxes and similar packaging for light cardboard, manila folders for card stock paper, leftover pieces of wrapping paper, and so forth. This not only reduces the cost of the projects but is also a great way to reuse and recycle paper. Be sure to ask an adult for permission before using any recycled paper products.

The projects in this book were created for this particular holiday. However, I invite readers to be imaginative and find new ways to use the ideas in this book to create different projects of their own. Please feel free to share pictures of your work with me through www.mcgeeproductions.com. Happy Crafting!

EASTER!

Winter held the land in its icy grip, freezing the forests and fields. Eostre, a goddess full of light and life, used her powers to loosen winter's hold over the land. She sent her messenger, the rabbit, to leave eggs around the homes of the humans as symbols of new life, to let them know that spring was on its way. Soon the land came to life again; leaves sprouted on trees, flowers bloomed, eggs hatched, and birds sang.

This is an ancient German myth about the coming of spring. The

word *Easter* is based on the name "Eostre." The rabbit or bunny and eggs became important symbols in Germany for the Easter holiday. Areas of Germany and eastern Europe are known for their elaborately dyed and painted Easter eggs. Children built little nests of grass in their caps or bonnets for the Easter bunny to place its eggs and treats, but soon baskets replaced the caps and bonnets.

German, Polish, and other European settlers to the United States brought with them their traditions of Easter rabbits, decorated eggs, and baskets of treats. During the late 1860s, many Americans started sharing in the fun traditions of their new European neighbors. Chocolate bunnies and eggs are now very popular treats to receive on Easter. More than ninety million chocolate bunnies are sold each year.

There are large Easter parades in many North American cities and contests for the most beautiful Easter hats or bonnets. Many North Americans celebrate Easter with rabbits, eggs, and flowers; wearing bright, new clothes; attending church services; sharing treats in the shape of rabbits, eggs, and chicks; having Easter egg-rolling races; and having Easter egg hunts. In 1876, President Andrew Johnson had an Easter egg hunt for his family outside the White House in Washington, D.C., the home of the president of the United States. A few years later, the White House started the annual tradition of sponsoring a special Easter egg hunt and egg-rolling race on the South Lawn. You will not need to hunt for fun ideas for decorations to help you celebrate Easter; just turn the page!

TISSUE PAPER "PYSANKY" EGGS

WHAT YOU WILL NEED

- a hollowed egg or plastic egg
- pencil
- tracing paper
- tissue paper in various colors
- scissors
- white glue
- permanent marking pens

Pysanky (PEH-san-keh) is the art of decorating Easter eggs from the eastern European countries of Poland and the Ukraine. Traditionally the eggs are decorated in a long process that uses dyes and beeswax. Using tissue paper is easier and can give beautiful results. The colors used have special meanings: white = purity and light, yellow = sunshine and warmth, orange = strength, green means springtime and life, red = charity and hope, blue = the skies and truth, and purple = faith.

WHAT TO DO

1. Use a hollowed real egg or plastic egg for your project. **Note:** Have an adult help you if you hollow a real egg. Use a large sewing needle to poke a small hole in the small end of the egg. Poke a larger hole, about the size of a pea, in the large end of the egg. Have an adult blow against the small hole until the egg white and yolk are forced out the larger hole in the bottom. Save the egg white and yolk in a bowl for use in cooking. Rinse the hollow egg with water and let it dry on a paper towel.

2. Use a pencil and tracing paper to transfer the patterns on page 37 to the tissue paper. Cut several shapes from different colors of tissue paper to decorate the egg.

3. Use a little white glue to fasten the colored tissue paper designs on the egg in patterns as you wish. Let dry.

4. Use permanent marking pens to add little lines and borders to the colored tissue paper.

5. Place your pysanky egg on an Easter egg stand. (See page 9 on how to make an egg stand.)

Easter Egg Stands

What you will need

- toilet tissue tube
- scissors
- pencil
- tracing paper
- construction paper—various colors
- white glue
- glitter glue
- markers or crayons
- sequins or craft jewels (optional)
- decorated eggs

Easter eggs can be very beautiful, but they are also fragile. You may want to display your specially decorated eggs in a way that will keep them from getting cracked accidentally. You need an Easter egg stand to hold up your special egg for all to see.

WHAT TO DO

1. Cut the toilet tissue tube into one-inch lengths.

2. Use a pencil and tracing paper to transfer the base patterns from page 42 to the construction paper. There are different base patterns that you may choose from.

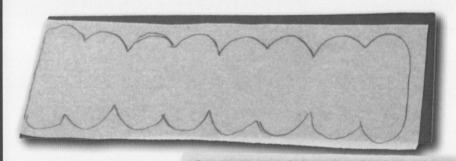

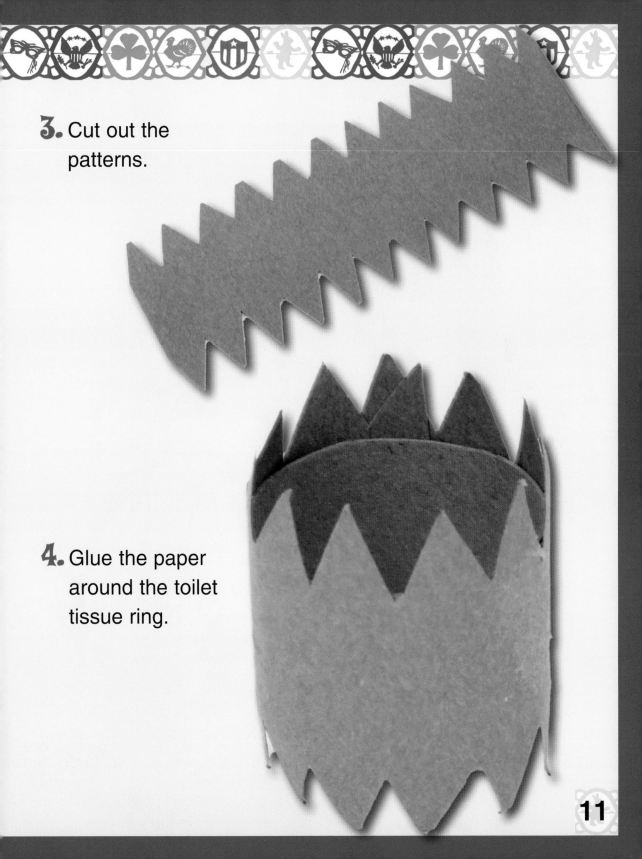

3. Cut out the patterns.

4. Glue the paper around the toilet tissue ring.

5. Decorate the ring with markers or crayons, pieces of colored paper, glitter glue, and sequins or craft jewels as you wish.

6. Fold the paper on the dotted lines as indicated and set it flat on a table. Place the decorated egg on the stand.

Easter Lily Pop-up Card

The beautiful white Easter lily is another popular symbol of the Easter holiday. The lily blooms in early spring. Tradition says that the pure white flowers symbolize purity. Many people give lilies as gifts and use them as decorations in their homes and churches. More than 12 million Easter lily bulbs are sent to markets every year.

What you will need

- white card stock
- pencil
- tracing paper
- scissors
- markers or crayons
- white glue
- construction paper— any color

What to do

1. Fold the white card stock in half width-wise, like a book.

2. Use the tracing paper to transfer the pattern from page 40 to the card stock.

3. Cut along the solid black lines of the pattern.

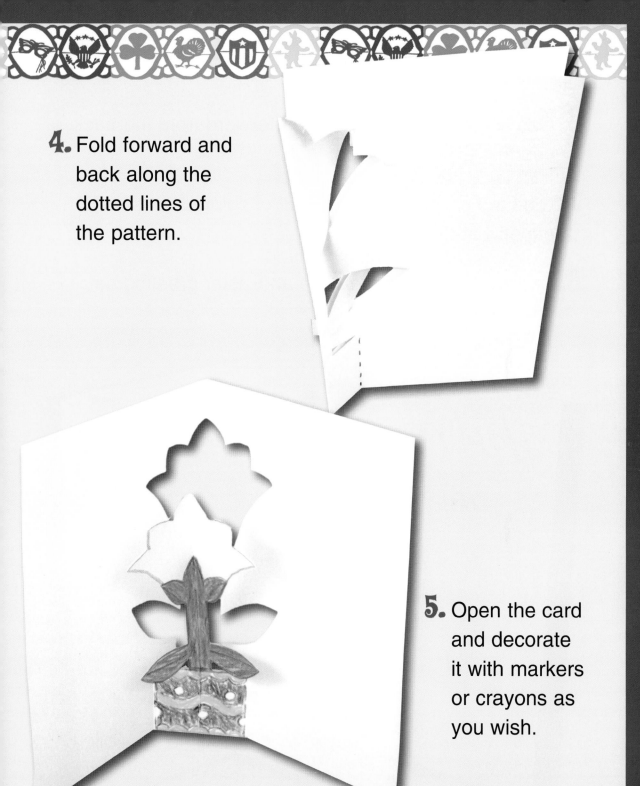

4. Fold forward and back along the dotted lines of the pattern.

5. Open the card and decorate it with markers or crayons as you wish.

6. Gently push the flower design forward from the back and fold the card closed.

7. Glue the card stock to a piece of colored construction paper. Let dry.

8. Decorate the card and write an Easter greeting as you wish.

BUNNY EARS

The rabbit has been a symbol for Easter since ancient times. In 1950, the famous singer Gene Autry recorded a song called "Here Comes Peter Cottontail," which claimed that Peter Cottontail was the one and only Easter bunny. So put on your bunny ears and jump in there with Peter to celebrate Easter!

WHAT YOU WILL NEED

- ✎ poster board— 14 x 11 inches
- ✎ pencil
- ✎ tracing paper
- ✎ scissors
- ✎ markers or crayons

WHAT TO DO

1. Fold the poster board in half width-wise, like a book.

2. Use a pencil and tracing paper to transfer the pattern on page 43 to the poster board.

17

3. Cut out the pattern along the solid lines.

4. Lay the pattern out flat before you and decorate it as you wish with the markers or crayons.

5. Gently push the bottom of the ears back and slip it on your head.

Funny Bunnies and Kooky Chicks

There are lots of fun activities associated with Easter. Coloring eggs, Easter egg hunts, and rolling egg races are just a few of such activities. What are some Easter activities or games you like? Make some funny bunnies and kooky chicks playing their favorite Easter games!

What you will need

- pencil
- tracing paper
- card stock—assorted colors
- scissors
- air-drying modeling material
- toothpicks
- little beads or small plastic jewels—dark color
- cotton swab
- markers
- watercolors

WHAT TO DO

1. Use the pencil and tracing paper to transfer the patterns from page 39 to the card stock and cut out the pieces.

2. Divide the air-drying modeling material into two balls, one the size of a cherry and the other the size of a walnut.

3. While the modeling material is still soft, use half of the toothpick to fasten the smaller ball on top of the larger ball. Be careful with the toothpicks, as some have sharp points.

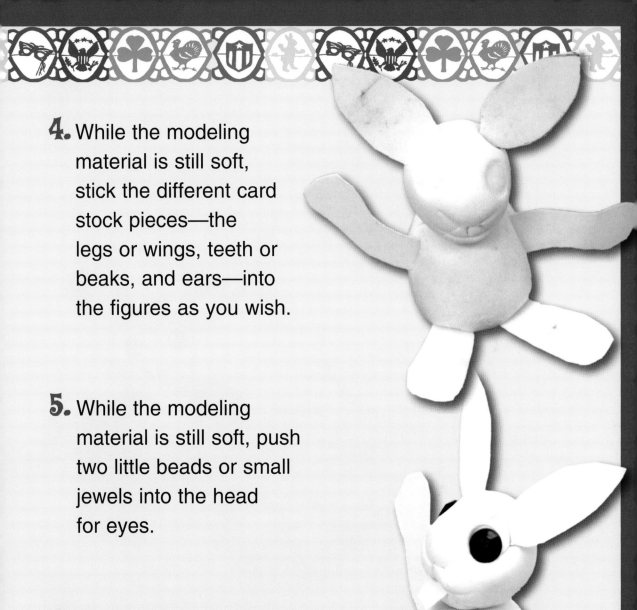

4. While the modeling material is still soft, stick the different card stock pieces—the legs or wings, teeth or beaks, and ears—into the figures as you wish.

5. While the modeling material is still soft, push two little beads or small jewels into the head for eyes.

6. Cut the cotton tip off of a cotton swab and place it as the tail on the rabbit. Let the modeling material dry.

7. Use colored markers or watercolors to decorate the figures.

Happy Hatching Chick

What you will need

- eggshell
- pencil
- tracing paper
- construction paper (yellow, orange, and green)
- scissors
- markers or crayons
- white glue
- Easter grass (optional)

Eggs have always been an important part of Easter traditions. The egg has symbolized the promise of new life to many cultures over the centuries. An egg seems to be a lifeless object and yet life bursts forth when a chick hatches. The chick is cute and lively soon after it hatches from its egg.

WHAT TO DO

1. Have an adult help you get half an eggshell. Be sure that it has been rinsed clean and dried. Set it aside where it will not get broken.

2. Use a pencil and tracing paper to transfer the chick pattern from page 41 to the yellow construction paper. Transfer the beak pattern from page 41 to the orange construction paper.

3. Cut out the patterns from the construction paper.

4. Lay the chick pattern out flat and decorate it with markers or crayons as you wish.

5. Glue the beak in place with a small drop of white glue. Let dry.

6. Fold the pattern on the dotted lines and glue the little flap just under the chick's head. Let dry.

7. Glue the chick to the inside of the eggshell with a drop of white glue.

8. Gently glue the eggshell to a green construction paper base. Add Easter grass around the egg as you wish.

Easter Place Mats

Lent is observed by many churches as a time of fasting, which means that some meals are purposely missed or certain foods are not eaten. Easter marks the end of Lent.

What you will need

- pencil
- tracing paper
- construction paper— 12 x 18 inches in various colors
- scissors
- white glue
- markers or crayons

Many families celebrate the end of Lent with an Easter feast. In many countries, children wake up on Easter morning to find a basket full of treats, eggs, and other surprises. This Easter place mat can be set out for your Easter basket or as a place setting for your Easter feast.

WHAT TO DO

1. Use a pencil and
tracing paper to
transfer the designs
from page 38 to a
12 x 18-inch sheet of purple
construction paper.

Note: You may use any three colors you wish, but in
this example, we are using purple, white, and green.

2. Cut along the solid lines of the patterns.

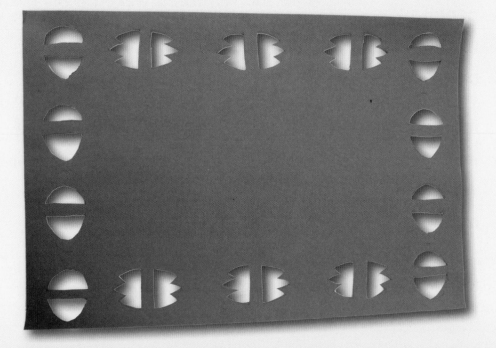

3. Cut two
1 ½ x 18-inch
strips of white
construction
paper and two
1 ½ x 18-inch strips of green construction paper.

4. Carefully weave the green paper strips through the designs you cut along the long sides of the purple construction paper.

5. Carefully weave the white paper strips through the designs you cut in the short sides of the purple construction paper. Trim and decorate the white ends that stick out as you wish.

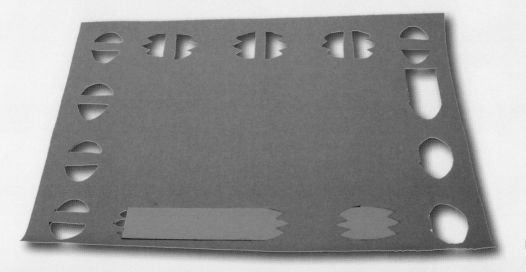

6. Use a drop of white glue to secure the strips in place at the corners.

7. Decorate the place mats with markers or crayons as you wish.

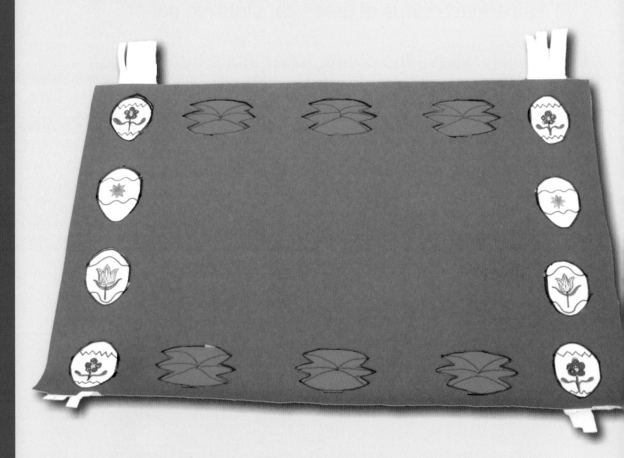

Paper "Stained Glass" Windows

During the day, the sunlight makes stained glass windows glow on the inside, and during the night, the electric lights make them glow on the outside. They can be found in many churches. Their bright colors, beautiful scenes and symbols, and noble characters help to uplift and inspire people. Stained glass windows have appeared in churches since 450 CE. The people who make these works of art use colored glass and lead, and they put them together like a giant puzzle.

What You Will Need

- rolled craft paper (bulletin board paper) black—8 x 8 inches
- pencil
- tracing paper
- scissors
- glue stick
- tissue paper— various colors
- white glue

WHAT TO DO

1. Fold the 8 x 8-inch black craft paper into a 4 x 4-inch square.

2. Use pencil and tracing paper to copy the pattern from page 36 onto black craft paper.

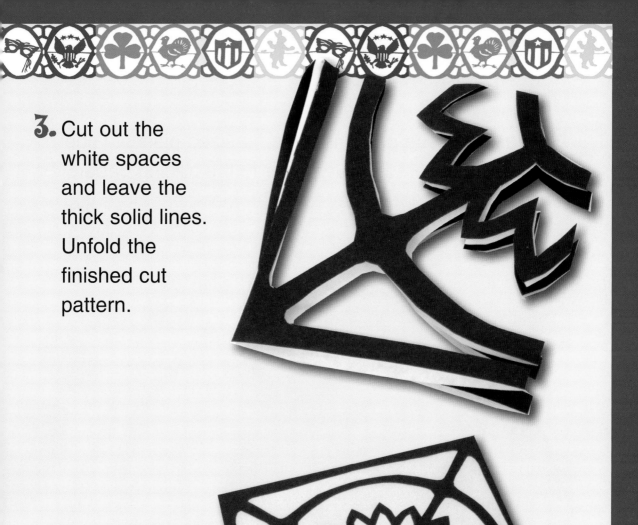

3. Cut out the white spaces and leave the thick solid lines. Unfold the finished cut pattern.

4. Use a glue stick to glue a sheet of tracing paper to one side of the black paper design. Let dry.

5. Tear the tissue paper into stamp-sized pieces. Glue pieces of colored tissue paper to the tracing paper, covering the open spaces of the black paper as you wish. Let dry.

6. Have an adult help you hang your stained glass
window in a place that will catch the light.

PATTERNS

The percentages included on the patterns tell you how much to enlarge or shrink the image using a copier. Most copiers and printers have an adjustable size/percentage feature to change the size of an image when you print it. After you print the patterns to their true sizes, cut them out or use tracing paper to copy them. Ask an adult to help you trace and cut the shapes.

Stained Glass Pattern

Place dotted line on the fold of the paper.

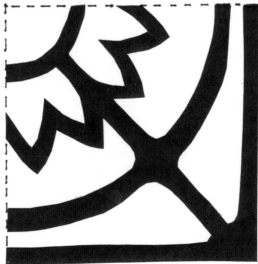

At 100%

Pysanky Egg Pattern

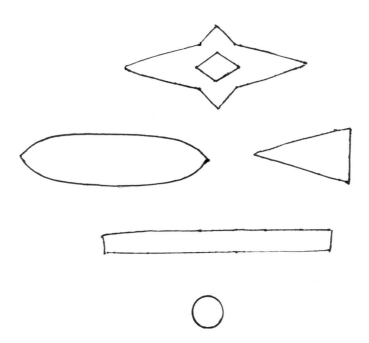

Reduce 50%

Easter Place Mat Pattern

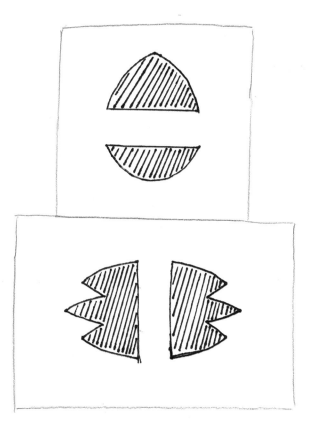

At 100%

Funny Bunny and Kooky Chick Pattern

Bunny Pieces

teeth
cut 1

ear
cut 2

paw
cut 2

foot
cut 2

Chick Pieces

beak
cut 1

foot
cut 2

wing
cut 2

At 100%

39

Lily Pop-up Card

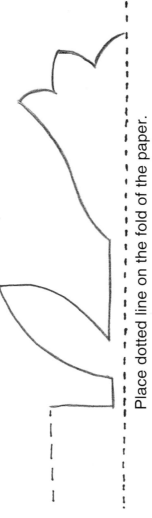

Place dotted line on the fold of the paper.

At 100%

Happy Hatching Chick

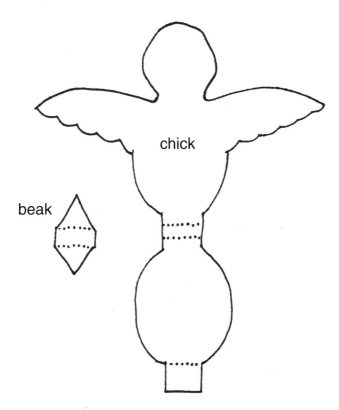

beak

chick

At 100%

Easter Egg Stands

At 100%

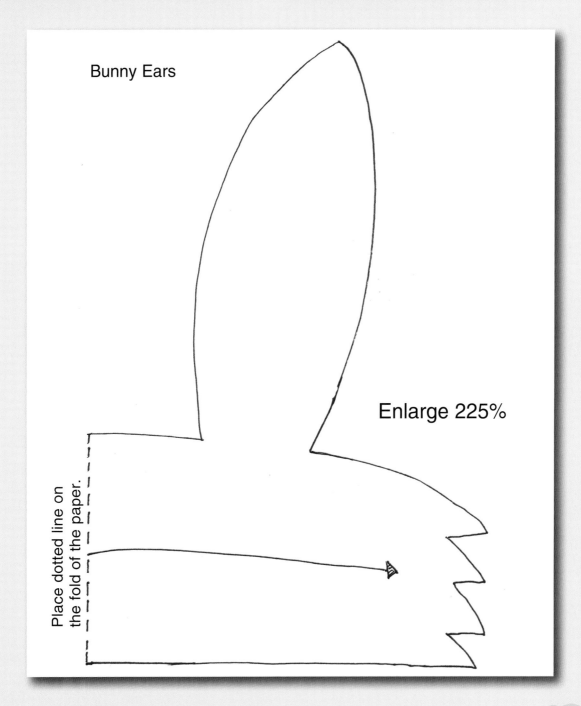

Bunny Ears

Enlarge 225%

Place dotted line on
the fold of the paper.

43

READ ABOUT

Books

Peppas, Lynn. *Easter.* New York: Crabtree Pub. Co., 2009.

Pfeffer, Wendy. *A New Beginning: Celebrating the Spring Equinox.* New York: Dutton Children's Books, 2008.

Trueit, Trudi Strain. *Easter.* Mankato, Minn.: Child's World, 2008.

Internet Addresses

EasterBunny's.Net: Easter Traditions

<http://www.easterbunnys.net/traditions.htm>

Kaboose: Easter Crafts

<http://crafts.kaboose.com/
  holidays/easter/>

**DLTK's: Easter Activities
for Children**

<http://www.dltk-holidays.com/
  easter/index.html>

Visit Randel McGee's Web site at
<http://www.mcgeeproductions.com>

INDEX

ABOUT THE AUTHOR

Randel McGee has been playing with paper and scissors for as long as he can remember. As soon as he was able to get a library card, he would go to the library and find the books that showed paper crafts, check them out, take them home, and try almost every craft in the book. He still checks out books on paper crafts at the library, but he also buys books to add to his own library and researches paper-craft sites on the Internet.

McGee says, "I begin by making copies of simple crafts or designs I see in books. Once I get the idea of how something is made, I begin to make changes to make the designs more personal. After a lot of trial and error, I find ways to do something new and different that is all my own. That's when the fun begins!"

McGee has also liked singing and acting from a young age. He graduated from college with a degree in children's theater and specialized in puppetry. After college, he taught himself ventriloquism and started performing at libraries and schools with a friendly dragon puppet named Groark. "Randel McGee and Groark" have toured throughout the

United States and Asia, sharing their fun shows with young and old alike. Groark is the star of two award-winning video series for elementary school students on character education: *Getting Along With Groark* and *The Six Pillars of Character.*

In the 1990s, McGee combined his love of making things with paper with his love of telling stories. He tells stories while making pictures cut from paper to illustrate the tales he tells. The famous author Hans Christian Andersen also made cut-paper pictures when he told stories. McGee portrays Andersen in storytelling performances around the world.

Besides performing and making things, McGee, with the help of his wife, Marsha, likes showing librarians, teachers, fellow artists, and children the fun and educational experiences they can have with paper crafts, storytelling, drama, and puppetry. Randel McGee has belonged to the Guild of American Papercutters, the National Storytelling Network, and the International Ventriloquists' Association. He has been a regional director for the Puppeteers of America, Inc., and past president of UNIMA-USA, an international puppetry organization. He has been active in working with children and scouts in his community and church for many years. He and his wife live in California. They are the parents of five grown children who are all talented artists and performers.